D1630091

44139001514169

The Jan Pieńkowski Nursery Books:
Colours, Faces, Food, Homes, Numbers,
Shapes, Time, Weather, Wheels, Yes No

for Lucretia

This edition published 2009 by Walker Books Ltd
87 Vauxhall Walk, London SE11 5HJ
10 9 8 7 6 5 4 3 2 1
© 1986, 2009 Jan Pieńkowski

The moral rights of the author/illustrator have been asserted
Lettering by Caroline Austin

Printed in China All rights reserved
British Library Cataloguing in Publication Data is available
ISBN 978-1-4063-1434-2 www.walker.co.uk

WALKER BOOKS
AND SUBSIDIARIES

LONDON • BOSTON • SYDNEY • AUCKLAND

FOOD

Jan Pieńkowski

milk

egg

bread

honey

fish

sausages

rice

chocolate

banana

potatoes

ice cream